10 COMMANDMENTS FOR BUILDING HEALTHY RELATIONSHIPS

For Single and Married People

Dr. Anthony Walton

Shirley Walton

10 COMMANDMENTS FOR BUILDING HEALTHY RELATIONSHIPS

ISBN: 978-1-7367209-7-4

Walton Publishing
Indianapolis, Indiana 46226
waltonpublishing@att.net

Printed in USA

DEDICATION

I dedicate this book to my dear sister Brenda Kaye Walton Morris. Brenda was a very kind and loving sister whose faith in God was relentless as she held on to the word of God believing that there was no wavering in His word.

Brenda was kind and supportive of whoever was in need, whether blessing them materially or sharing a powerful word from God.

You are gone from us; you will forever be remembered and in our hearts.

Next, I dedicate this book to those who are seeking to have meaningful God-centered relationships. May you find and experience the Agape love that God has designed for you to experience.

Table of Contents

Author's note:

Throughout this book you will find "Positive Affirmations" which have been included as a resource to remind the reader to see their circumstances with a more optimistic view.

Positive Affirmation

I possess the ability to make my dreams and aspirations a reality.

This affirmation reminds you that you have the potential and the necessary skills to transform your dreams and goals into tangible achievements. It encourages you to take action and believe in your capacity to succeed.

Purpose

The purpose of writing this book is to give those who are serious about maintaining a God-centered relationship the tools to do so.

I talk with many Christians who are in unhealthy relationships, whether it be church, family, work, or even marriage. Many of these relationships are on life support with the person or persons involved struggling to maintain any kind of positive relationship.

I believe for many of those struggling with relationship issues given the proper tools can find themselves on their way to a happy, enriched, and God-centered relationship.

I hope that after reading this book the reader will see it as a spiritual tool to help them to better the various relationships they may encounter.

There are a number of topics in this book that should cover whatever challenges most Christians will find themselves facing in their relationships.

Positive Affirmation

**I have faith in my capabilities and
trust the strength within me.**

This affirmation emphasizes self-belief and self-trust.
It encourages you to rely on your inner strength and
abilities to face challenges and make the right
decisions.

Introduction

In the complex journey of relationships, we often encounter many complexities along with a series of highs and lows, moments of jubilation, as well as challenges that test our ability to love. These fluctuations are a natural part of the very fiber of love. They serve as valuable lessons, shaping and strengthening the connections to others that we hold dear.

Our communication also plays a pivotal role in addressing the hurdles that may surface in any relationship. Open and effective dialogue serves as a powerful tool in resolving issues and fostering understanding between others.

Trust, which is a cornerstone of all relationships, is fragile. It can be compromised and restoring it once it has been damaged can be difficult, if not almost impossible to rebuild. Rebuilding trust requires patience, commitment, and effort from all parties involved.

It is essential to recognize that every relationship, regardless of its nature, will encounter its share of difficulties. However, it is not the presence of these challenges but how we choose to navigate through them that truly defines the resilience and strength of the bond.

Positive Affirmation

**I can do all things through Christ
who strengthens me.**

~ Philippians 4:13

This affirmation emphasizes your capability to achieve
your dreams and goals through the strength provided by
your faith in Christ.

What are the 10 Commandments?

The Ten Commandments, also known as the Decalogue, are a set of ethical and moral principles found in the Bible, specifically in the Book of Exodus and the Book of Deuteronomy. These commandments are considered foundational in both Judaism and Christianity. Here are the traditional Ten Commandments:

1. You shall have no other gods before me.

2. You shall not make for yourself an idol or worship any other gods.

3. You shall not take the name of the Lord your God in vain.

4. Remember the Sabbath day and keep it holy.

5. Honor your father and mother.

6. You shall not murder.

7. You shall not commit adultery.

8. You shall not steal.

9. You shall not bear false witness against your neighbor (i.e., you shall not lie).

10. You shall not covet anything that belongs to your neighbor.

Positive Affirmation

I display resilience, conquering challenges with grace and determination.

Resilience is a key quality in achieving victory in life. This affirmation reinforces your ability to gracefully overcome obstacles with determination and a positive attitude.

10 Reasons Why Having God in Your Relationships is Important

1. **Shared Values and Beliefs:**

   A common faith can provide a strong foundation of shared values and beliefs that guide the relationship.

2. **Spiritual Connection:**

   A spiritual connection can deepen emotional intimacy and create a sense of purpose in the relationship.

   "The Seven Principles for Making Marriage Work" by Dr. John Gottman.

3. **Guidance in Difficult Times:**

   Belief in a higher power can offer comfort, guidance, and strength during challenging moments in the relationship.

4. **Forgiveness and Redemption:**

   Faith often emphasizes forgiveness and redemption, which can be crucial in resolving conflicts and moving forward.

   "Forgiveness: Letting Go of Grudges and Bitterness" (Mayo Clinic, 2018).

5. **Moral Compass:**

   A shared faith can serve as a moral compass, helping couples make ethical decisions and maintain integrity.

   "The Ethics of What We Eat" by Peter Singer and Jim Mason (2007)

6. Community Support:

Religious communities provide a support network of like-minded individuals who can offer guidance and encouragement.

"The Importance of Religious Community" by PositivePsychology.com (2020).

7. Coping with Loss:

Belief in God can provide solace and meaning when dealing with loss or grief in the relationship.

"A Grief Observed" by C.S. Lewis (1961).

8. Prayer and Reflection:

Joint prayer and spiritual reflection can be a bonding experience that enhances the relationship.

9. Marriage and Family Values:

Faith often emphasizes the sanctity of marriage and family, reinforcing commitment.

10. Hope and Resilience:

Belief in God can foster hope and resilience, helping couples navigate challenges with optimism.

"The Resilience Factor" by Karen Reivich and Andrew Shatté (2003).

"My son, keep thy father's commandment and forsake not the law of thy mother: Bind them continually upon thine heart, and tie them about thy neck" ~ Proverbs 6:20-21 KJV

Examples of the 10 Commandments in Relationships

1. You shall have no other gods before me.

   Example:
   Prioritizing your partner's emotional needs over spending excessive time at work or with friends.

2. You shall not make for yourself an idol or worship any other gods.

   Example:
   Not becoming obsessed with material possessions or a hobby to the point that you neglect spending time with your partner.

3. You shall not take the name of the Lord your God in vain.

   Example:
   Avoiding disrespectful or hurtful language during disagreements and maintaining a civil tone when communicating with your partner.

4. Remember the Sabbath day and keep it holy.

   Example:
   Setting aside regular date nights or weekends to focus exclusively on your relationship, away from work or other distractions.

5. Honor your father and mother.

   Example:
   Respecting and being considerate of your partner's parents and family, even if you have differences with them.

6. You shall not murder.

Example:
Never physically harming or emotionally abusing your partner during conflicts or disagreements.

7. You shall not commit adultery.

Example:
Maintaining fidelity and trust in your relationship, refraining from engaging in romantic or sexual affairs outside of your partnership.

8. You shall not steal.

Example:
Respecting your partner's privacy and personal boundaries, refraining from taking or using their possessions without permission.

9. You shall not bear false witness against your neighbor (i.e., you shall not lie).

Example:
Being honest and transparent with your partner, even when it's difficult, and not deceiving or lying to them.

10. You shall not covet anything that belongs to your neighbor.

Example:
Avoid jealousy or envy when your partner achieves success or has positive experiences, instead celebrate their achievements and happiness.

"Wherefore the law is holy, and the commandment holy, and just, and good."   ~ *Romans 7:12*

10 Ways Singles Can Connect
With Other Singles

Connecting with others when you're single can be an enriching experience that leads to new friendships, romantic relationships, and personal growth. Here are 10 ways singles can connect with others:

1. **Online Dating:**

   Explore various online dating platforms, such as Tinder, Bumble, Match.com, or OkCupid. Create a compelling profile that showcases your personality, interests, and what you're looking for in a relationship. Engage in meaningful conversations with potential matches and consider virtual or in-person dates to get to know them better.

2. **Join Social Groups:**
   Identify social groups or clubs that align with your hobbies and interests. Whether you're into hiking, book clubs, photography, or board games, there are likely local groups or online communities where you can meet like-minded people. Websites like Meetup.com are excellent resources for finding these groups.

3. **Attend Events:**
   Keep an eye out for local events happening in your area, such as music festivals, food fairs, art exhibitions, or conventions. These events provide opportunities to meet people who share your enthusiasm for the same activities.

4. Volunteer:

Volunteering is a wonderful way to connect with others while giving back to your community. Find a cause or organization that resonates with you, and offer your time and skills. You'll meet people who are passionate about similar causes, which can be a strong basis for friendship.

5. Take Classes:

Enroll in classes or workshops that interest you. Whether it's learning a new language, taking up a cooking class, or attending a dance workshop, these environments provide a conducive setting for meeting individuals who share your desire for personal growth and skill development.

6. Utilize Social Media:

Connect with people on social media platforms like Facebook, Twitter, or Instagram who share your interests. Engage in conversations, participate in online communities, and attend virtual events or webinars that align with your passions.

7. Professional Networking:

Join professional organizations or attend networking events in your field. Not only can this boost your career prospects, but it can also introduce you to like-minded individuals who share your career goals and interests.

8. Join Meetup Groups:

Explore platforms like Meetup.com, where you can find a wide range of local groups and events catering to diverse interests. These groups may include hiking clubs, wine enthusiasts, tech enthusiasts, or singles' meetups.

9. Travel and Adventure:

Embrace your adventurous side by traveling solo or joining group travel tours. Traveling allows you to meet people from various backgrounds and cultures, broadening your horizons and providing opportunities for unique connections.

10. Attend Speed Dating or Singles' Events:

Keep an eye out for local speed dating events, singles' mixers, or themed parties designed for singles. These events are specifically organized for people looking to connect with potential partners in a relaxed and fun atmosphere.

Remember that building connections with others is not limited to finding a romantic partner. Creating a robust social network can lead to meaningful friendships, personal development, and support in various aspects of your life. Be open to new experiences, take the initiative to engage with others, and always be true to yourself, as authenticity is key in forming genuine and lasting connections.

Positive Affirmation

**I trust in the Lord with all my heart
and lean not on my understanding**

~ Proverbs 3:5

This affirmation encourages trust in God's
wisdom and your faith in His abilities.

Relating The 10 Commandments to Relationships

1. **You shall have no other gods before me.**

   In a relationship, prioritize your partner and the relationship itself, valuing it above all else.

2. **You shall not make for yourself an idol or worship any other gods.**

   Avoid putting material possessions, career, or other personal pursuits above your partner and the commitment you share.

3. **You shall not take the name of the Lord your God in vain.**

   Show respect and consideration for your partner, refraining from using hurtful or disrespectful language.

4. **Remember the Sabbath day and keep it holy.**

   Set aside dedicated time for your relationship, fostering quality time together and allowing for rest and rejuvenation as a couple.

5. **Honor your father and mother.**

   Treat each other's families with respect and consideration, recognizing the importance of your partner's family ties.

6. **You shall not murder.**

Avoid any physical or emotional harm to your partner. This includes not only physical violence but also hurtful words or actions.

7. **You shall not commit adultery.**

Stay faithful and committed to your partner, both emotionally and physically.

8. **You shall not steal.**

Respect each other's boundaries, possessions, and personal space. Avoid dishonesty and theft in any form.

9. **You shall not bear false witness against your neighbor (i.e., you shall not lie).**

Be truthful and honest with your partner, as trust is essential for a healthy relationship.

You shall not covet anything that belongs to your neighbor.

10. **Avoid jealousy and envy within the relationship.**

Focus on contentment with what you have and appreciating your partner's qualities and efforts.

"The law of the Lord is perfect, reviving the soul; the testimony of the Lord is sure, making wise the simple; the precepts of the Lord are right, rejoicing the heart; the commandment of the Lord is pure, enlightening the eyes; the fear of the Lord is clean, enduring forever; the rules of the Lord are true, and righteous altogether."
~ Psalms 19:7-9 KJV

Quotes Related to the 10 Commandments

1. "Love does not begin and end the way we seem to think it does. Love is a Battle; Love is a War; Love is a Growing Up." - James Baldwin Source: "The Fire Next Time" by James Baldwin (1963)

2. "Do not love the world or anything in the world. If anyone loves the world, love for the Father is not in them." *I John 2:15-16 (New Testament, Bible)*

3. "A good marriage allows for change and growth in the individuals and in the way they express their love." - Pearl S. Buck Source: "The Good Earth" by Pearl S. Buck (1931)

4. "The best thing to hold onto in life is each other." - Audrey Hepburn Source: Various interviews and public statements by Audrey Hepburn.

5. "To lose one parent may be regarded as a misfortune; to lose both looks like carelessness." - Oscar Wilde Source: "The Importance of Being Earnest" by Oscar Wilde (1895)

6. "Hatred paralyzes life; love releases it. Hatred confuses life; love harmonizes it. Hatred darkens life; love illuminates it." - Martin Luther King Jr. Source: Various speeches and writings by Martin Luther King Jr.

7. "I have waited for this opportunity for more than half a century, to repeat to you once again my vow of eternal fidelity and everlasting love." - Gabriel Garcia Marquez Source: "Love in the Time of Cholera" by Gabriel Garcia Marquez (1985)

8. "The great gift of human beings is that we have the power of empathy." - Meryl Streep Source: Various interviews and public statements by Meryl Streep.

9. "The truth is rarely pure and never simple." - Oscar Wilde Source: "The Importance of Being Earnest" by Oscar Wilde (1895)

10. "Comparison is the thief of joy." - Theodore Roosevelt Source: Various speeches and writings by Theodore Roosevelt.

"The law of the Lord is perfect, converting the soul: the testimony of the Lord is sure, making wise the simple."
~ Psalms 19:7 KJV

10 Warning Signs of
an Unhealthy Relationship

Recognizing warning signs of an unhealthy relationship is crucial for your emotional and physical well-being.

1. Lack of Trust:

A healthy relationship is built on trust. If you constantly doubt your partner or feel they don't trust you, it's a warning sign.

2. Constant Criticism:

Regularly being criticized or demeaned by your partner can be emotionally damaging. In a healthy relationship, constructive feedback is given with care and respect.

3. Isolation:

If your partner discourages you from spending time with friends and family, it's a sign of control and manipulation, which is unhealthy.

4. Excessive Jealousy:

Occasional jealousy is normal, but if your partner is excessively jealous or tries to control who you interact with, it's a warning sign of an unhealthy relationship.

5. **Verbal or Physical Abuse:**

Any form of abuse, be it verbal, physical, or emotional, is a clear sign of an unhealthy relationship. Seek help and support if you are in this situation.

6. **Lack of Respect:**

Respect is a fundamental aspect of a healthy relationship. If your partner disrespects your boundaries, opinions, or feelings, it's a serious problem.

7. **Constant Arguments:**

Frequent, unresolved, or intense arguments can be a sign of underlying issues in the relationship. In a healthy partnership, conflicts are managed constructively.

8. **Gaslighting:**

Gaslighting involves manipulating or distorting your reality, making you doubt your own perceptions and memory. It's a form of emotional abuse and a significant warning sign.

9. **Emotional Neglect:**

Emotional neglect involves a lack of emotional support, empathy, and validation from your partner. It can lead to feelings of loneliness and unhappiness.

10. **Unequal Power Dynamics:**

An unhealthy relationship may have unequal power dynamics, with one partner exerting control and dominance over the other. Equality and mutual respect are key to a healthy relationship.

If you recognize these warning signs in your relationship, it's essential to seek help, either through therapy, counseling or by talking to a trusted friend or family member. In some cases, the best option may be to end the relationship if it is consistently harmful or abusive. Your safety and well-being should always be a top priority.

Positive Affirmation

**I naturally draw success and
opportunities into my life**

This affirmation promotes the idea that a positive mindset
and self-belief can attract success and opportunities. It
encourages you to expect and recognize these opportunities
as they come your way.

10 Ways to Establish Better Worship with Your Spouse or Family

1. **Pray Together:**

   Regularly pray together as a couple. Joint prayer can deepen your spiritual connection and strengthen your bond. "Prayer: Experiencing Awe and Intimacy with God" by Timothy Keller (2014).

2. **Study Scripture Together:**

   Engage in Bible study or spiritual reading together. This shared learning experience can foster spiritual growth as a couple. Source: "The Bible" (Various translations).

3. **Attend Worship Services:**

   Attend religious services, such as church, mosque, or temple, together to worship as a couple and connect with your faith community. Source: Your respective place of worship.

4. **Share Spiritual Goals:**

   Discuss your spiritual goals and aspirations as a couple. Aligning your spiritual journeys can enhance your connection. Source: "The Seven Habits of Highly Effective People" by Stephen R. Covey (1989).

5. **Practice Gratitude:**

   Express gratitude together for your blessings and the love you share. Gratitude is a spiritual practice that can strengthen your relationship. Source: "The Psychology of Gratitude" by Robert A. Emmons and Michael E. McCullough (2004).

6. **Serve Together:**

   Volunteer or engage in acts of kindness as a couple, reflecting your shared values and beliefs. Source: Your chosen service opportunities.

7. **Discuss Faith Questions:**

   Engage in meaningful conversations about your faith, doubts, and questions. Honest discussions can lead to a deeper understanding of each other's beliefs.

8. **Forgive and Seek Forgiveness:**

   Practice forgiveness and seek forgiveness when needed. This aligns with many religious teachings and promotes harmony in your relationship.

9. **Celebrate Religious Holidays:**

   Celebrate religious holidays and traditions together, reinforcing your shared faith and creating meaningful memories.

10. **Seek Spiritual Guidance:**

    When facing challenges or seeking spiritual growth, consider seeking guidance from a trusted spiritual leader or counselor.

"Jesus said unto him, Thou shalt love the Lord thy God with all thy heart, and with all thy soul, and with all thy mind. This is the first and great commandment."

Matthew 22:37-38 KJV

10 Ways to Support Others

1. Listen Actively:

When someone is talking to you, practice active listening. Give your full attention, ask clarifying questions, and show empathy. *Covey, S. R. (1989). "The 7 Habits of Highly Effective People."*

2. Offer Emotional Support:

Be there for others during difficult times. Show empathy, provide a shoulder to lean on, and offer words of encouragement. *Walton, Anthony (2017) "The Empty Quiver" A Journey from the Pain of Despair and Loss to Recovery, Hope and Victory*

3. Provide Practical Help:

Offer concrete assistance when needed, whether it's helping with chores, running errands, or providing childcare.

4. Offer Positive Feedback:

Acknowledge and appreciate the efforts and achievements of others. Positive feedback can boost confidence and motivation. Heath, C., & Heath, D. (2007). "Made to Stick: Why Some Ideas Survive and Others Die."

5. Respect Boundaries:

Respect personal boundaries and preferences. Ensure that the help you offer aligns with what the person actually needs. Cloud, H., & Townsend, J. (1992). "Boundaries: When to Say Yes, How to Say No to Take Control of Your Life."

6. Encourage Self-Care:

Promote self-care and well-being. Encourage individuals to prioritize their physical and mental health. Source: Burton, J. (2016). "The Self-Care Solution."

7. Offer a Listening Ear:

Be available to listen to others without judgment or interruption. Sometimes, people just need someone to talk to. Rogers, C. R. (1961). "On Becoming a Person."

8. Celebrate Achievements:

Celebrate the accomplishments and milestones of others, no matter how small they may seem.

9. Empower and Encourage:

Encourage individuals to pursue their goals and passions. Empower them to believe in themselves. Dweck, C. S. (2006). "Mindset: The New Psychology of Success."

10. Educate Yourself:

Learn about the challenges others may face, such as mental health issues or cultural differences, to better understand and support them.

"But whoso hath this world's good, and seeth his brother have need, and shutteth up his bowels of compassion from him, how dwelleth the love of God in him? My little children, let us not love in word, neither in tongue; but in deed and in truth." ~ 1 John 3:17-18 KJV

10 Positive Things that Can Contribute to a Healthy and Strong Marriage:

1. **Effective Communication:**

   Open and honest communication is vital. Listening and expressing feelings, needs, and concerns can help resolve conflicts and deepen understanding.

2. **Trust:**

   Trust is the foundation of any strong marriage. Building and maintaining trust through honesty and reliability is crucial.

3. **Quality Time Together:**

   Spend quality time together regularly to nurture your connection. Date nights, shared hobbies, and quality conversations can strengthen the bond.

4. **Respect:**

   Show respect for each other's opinions, boundaries, and individuality. Treat each other with kindness and consideration.

5. **Emotional Support:**

   Be there for each other during both happy and challenging times. Offer emotional support, empathy, and encouragement.

6. **Shared Values:**

   Having shared values and goals can provide a sense of unity and purpose in the relationship.

7. **Intimacy:**

   Physical and emotional intimacy are essential. Keep the romantic and affectionate aspects of your relationship alive.

8. **Conflict Resolution:**

   Disagreements are normal, but how you resolve them matters. Learn healthy conflict resolution techniques and compromise when needed.

9. **Teamwork:**

   Approach challenges and responsibilities as a team. Collaborate on household tasks, parenting, and financial decisions.

10. **Continuous Growth:**

    Encourage each other's personal growth and self-improvement. Support your partner's aspirations and be willing to grow together as a couple.

"Let your speech be always with grace, seasoned with salt, that ye may know how ye ought to answer every man."

Colossians 4:6 KJV

10 *Examples* of Things that Can Contribute to a Healthy and Strong Marriage

(From Previous List)
1. **Effective Communication:**

   Instead of bottling up frustration, a spouse might say, "I've noticed that we've been arguing more lately, and I'd like to discuss what's been bothering us."

2. **Trust:**

   Trust is built when one spouse promises to do something, like taking care of a household chore, and consistently follows through without reminders.

3. **Quality Time Together:**

   A couple might decide to have a weekly date night, where they go out for dinner and take time to reconnect without distractions.

4. **Respect:**

   Even in disagreement, showing respect can look like saying, "I see where you're coming from, and I appreciate your perspective, even though I disagree."

5. **Emotional Support:**

   During a tough time, one spouse may say to the other, "I'm here for you, and I want you to know that I support you emotionally through this."

6. Shared Values:

A couple might discuss their values around family and decide to prioritize spending holidays with both sets of parents to honor those values.

7. Intimacy:

Expressing physical intimacy can be as simple as holding hands, cuddling on the couch, or sharing an affectionate kiss before leaving for work.

8. Conflict Resolution:

When a disagreement arises, a couple could use "I" statements, such as, "I feel hurt when this happens, and I'd like to discuss how we can avoid it in the future."

9. Teamwork:

Sharing responsibilities might mean one spouse takes care of the children's school activities while the other handles grocery shopping and cooking.

10. Continuous Growth:

Encouraging personal growth might involve supporting a spouse who wants to take up a new hobby, offering encouragement, and even participating together.

"And be ye kind one to another, tenderhearted, forgiving one another, even as God for Christ's sake hath forgiven you." ~ Ephesians 4:32 KJV

10 Short Stories of Overcoming Challenges and Building Stronger Relationships

1. A Lifelong Lesson in Patience:

Sarah and John faced infertility issues. They sought therapy and support groups. After years of struggles, they adopted a child and realized their relationship had grown stronger through the process.

2. Healing After Betrayal:

Lisa discovered her spouse's affair. After a period of pain and counseling, they decided to work on rebuilding trust. They learned to communicate more openly and honestly, ultimately strengthening their bond.

3. Financial Ups and Downs:

Mark and Emily went through bankruptcy due to unforeseen medical bills. They attended financial counseling and learned to budget together. This challenge taught them resilience and financial responsibility.

4. Navigating a Long-Distance Relationship:

Sarah and David had to live in different countries for work. They maintained their connection through regular video calls, surprise visits, and prioritizing their time together when possible. Their relationship grew stronger despite the distance.

5. **Blended Family Success:**

After a difficult divorce, Lisa and Mike decided to blend their families. It was challenging at first, but they attended family therapy and worked on creating a harmonious home for all their children. Over time, their efforts paid off, and their relationships became stronger.

6. **Health Crisis and Support:**

Emma was diagnosed with a serious illness. Her partner, Alex, provided unwavering support and care throughout her treatment. This challenging time brought them even closer together, emphasizing the importance of compassion and love.

7. **Cultural Differences:**

Maria and James came from different cultural backgrounds. They faced challenges related to family expectations and traditions. Through open dialogue and compromise, they learned to appreciate and incorporate aspects of each other's cultures into their lives.

8. **Loss of a Child:**

After the loss of our child, my wife Shirley and I found solace in drawing closer to God. We leaned on each other for support, and, in the process, our connection deepened as we navigated the devastating painful journey of loss together.

9. Overcoming Addiction:

Chris struggled with addiction. With the unwavering support of his partner, Lisa, he sought rehabilitation and therapy. Through this challenging process, their relationship transformed into one built on trust, understanding, and sobriety.

10. A Second Chance at Love:

Rebecca and David reconnected after years of being apart. Both had experienced failed marriages. They decided to give love another chance, appreciating the lessons they had learned. Their relationship thrived as they embraced this new chapter in their lives.

"And above all things have fervent charity among yourselves: for charity shall cover the multitude of sins."
1 Peter 4:8 KJV

Positive Affirmation

In all things, I am more than a conqueror through Him who loved me.

~ Romans 8:37

This affirmation highlights your resilience and determination, relying on God's love and strength to overcome challenges.

10 Ways Finances Affect Relationships

Finances can have a significant impact on relationships, and the way they affect a relationship can vary depending on a variety of factors, including individual personalities, values, and circumstances. Here are some common ways in which finances can affect relationships:

1. **Communication and Transparency**:

   Open and honest communication about finances is crucial in any relationship. Couples need to discuss their financial goals, spending habits, debts, and income to ensure they are on the same page. Lack of communication or financial secrets can lead to mistrust and conflicts.

2. **Conflict and Stress**:

   Money-related issues are a leading cause of conflicts in relationships. Disagreements over spending, saving, and financial priorities can create stress and tension. Arguments about money can be emotionally charged and may escalate if not addressed effectively.

3. **Power Dynamics**:

   Financial disparities between partners can sometimes create power imbalances in a relationship. The partner with more financial resources may have more control over decisions, which can lead to resentment or a feeling of dependency in the other partner.

4. **Financial Goals and Values**:

Differences in financial goals and values can strain a relationship. For example, if one partner values saving for the future while the other prefers to live for the moment, it can lead to conflicts over spending decisions and long-term planning.

5. **Debt and Financial Responsibility**:

Debt, especially high levels of debt, can place a significant burden on a relationship. It may limit a couple's ability to achieve their shared goals, and disagreements can arise over how to manage and pay off debt.

6. **Income Inequality**:

Significant income disparities between partners can lead to feelings of inadequacy or resentment. The lower-earning partner may feel financial pressure, while the higher-earning partner may feel burdened by supporting the relationship.

7. **Life Transitions**:

Major life transitions, such as job loss, illness, or retirement, can have a profound impact on a relationship's financial dynamics. Adjusting to these changes can be challenging and may require adaptation and support from both partners.

8. **Financial Infidelity**:

Keeping financial secrets or engaging in financial infidelity, such as hidden spending or undisclosed debt, can erode trust in a relationship.

9. **Long-Term Planning**:

Couples need to plan for their financial future together, which includes retirement planning, estate planning, and setting financial goals as a team. Failure to align on these long-term plans can lead to dissatisfaction and uncertainty.

10. **External Pressures**:

Social and cultural factors can also influence how finances affect relationships. For example, societal expectations about gender roles and financial responsibilities can add additional stressors to a relationship.

In order to help counter the negative effects of finances on a relationship, it's important for couples to:

- **Communicate openly**: Regularly discuss financial matters and be honest about your financial situation, goals, and concerns.

- **Create a budget**: Develop a joint budget that reflects both partners' priorities and ensures that both are contributing to shared expenses.

- **Set financial goals together**: Collaborate on financial goals and plans for the future.

- **Seek professional help**: If financial issues become too overwhelming, consider consulting a financial advisor or therapist who specializes in relationships and finances.

- **Compromise and show empathy**: Understand that financial disagreements are common, and it's essential to find compromises and show empathy toward each other's perspectives.

Ultimately, how finances affect a relationship depends on how well couples navigate these challenges and work together to achieve financial harmony. Open communication, mutual respect, and a willingness to address financial issues as a team are crucial for maintaining a healthy and strong relationship.

10 Additional Ways Finances Affect Relationships

1. Economic Disparities:

Income disparities between partners can introduce a complex dynamic into a relationship. It may lead to feelings of inadequacy or resentment, especially if one partner earns significantly more than the other. The partner with the higher income might feel a sense of responsibility, which can affect their self-esteem and even lead to stress. Conversely, the lower-earning partner may feel financial pressure, and this can strain their self-worth and contribute to feelings of dependency.

2. Lifestyle Choices:

Financial resources play a vital role in shaping the lifestyle that a couple can afford. Disagreements over spending can arise when partners have differing views on what constitutes a reasonable expenditure. These disagreements can involve everything from daily expenses to larger investments like a home or vacations. Finding a middle ground that aligns with both partners' values and priorities is crucial.

3. Financial Trust:

Trust is the foundation of a healthy relationship, and financial dishonesty can erode it. Financial secrets, hidden spending, undisclosed debt, or undisclosed financial decisions can lead to mistrust and conflict. Open and honest communication about financial matters is essential for maintaining trust in a relationship.

4. **Stress and Conflict:**

Financial disagreements are a common source of stress and conflict in relationships. These conflicts can be emotionally charged, leading to heated arguments that may have a lasting impact on the partnership. Addressing these conflicts constructively through effective communication and compromise is crucial for maintaining relationship health.

5. **Power Imbalances:**

Financial disparities can create power imbalances within a relationship. The partner with greater financial resources may have more control over decisions related to spending, investments, and even lifestyle choices. This power dynamic can lead to feelings of inequality, and the partner with less financial control may feel disempowered.

6. **Debt Burden:**

Debt, especially when it is substantial, can place a significant burden on a relationship. Partners may find themselves working together to manage and pay off debt, which can strain their financial stability and ability to meet other shared goals. Differing attitudes toward debt and its management can further complicate the situation.

7. **Financial Compatibility:**

Differences in financial values and priorities can create tensions within a relationship. For example, one partner may prioritize saving for the future, while the other may prefer to enjoy life in the present. These disparities can lead to conflicts regarding financial goals, budgeting, and long-term planning.

8. **Major Life Transitions:**

Life transitions, such as job loss, illness, or retirement, can significantly impact a relationship's financial dynamics. Partners may need to adapt to changing financial circumstances, which can be challenging and stressful. Adjusting to these changes often requires mutual support and a reassessment of financial goals.

9. **Long-Term Planning:**

Couples need to plan for their financial future together, including retirement planning, estate planning, and other long-term financial goals. Failing to align on these plans can lead to dissatisfaction and uncertainty about the future. Collaborative long-term planning is essential for maintaining a strong financial foundation.

10. **External Influences:**

External factors, such as societal norms and expectations, can influence how finances affect relationships. For example, traditional gender roles and expectations about financial responsibilities can add extra pressure to a relationship and impact how financial decisions are made.

This list highlights the complex ways in which finances can influence relationships, emphasizing the importance of open communication, mutual understanding, and cooperation to address financial challenges and maintain a healthy and harmonious partnership.

Positive Affirmation

I maintain control over my thoughts and emotions, guiding them positively.

This affirmation emphasizes the importance of emotional intelligence and self-regulation. It encourages you to stay in control of your thoughts and emotions, ensuring they are aligned with your goals and well-being.

10 Lessons for Building a Financially Strong Relationship

1. **Open Communication About Finances:**

   Discussing financial goals, income, and expenses openly is essential. According to a study published in the "Journal of Family and Economic Issues," effective communication about money is linked to higher marital satisfaction (Dew, 2008).

2. **Set Shared Financial Goals:**

   Establishing common financial objectives and working together to achieve them can strengthen your financial bond. Research from the National Bureau of Economic Research shows that setting joint financial goals enhances financial outcomes in relationships (Botti, 2015).

3. **Budgeting and Expense Management:**

   Learning to budget and manage expenses as a team can improve financial stability. Websites like Investopedia provide valuable budgeting tips for couples (Investopedia).

4. **Emergency Fund:**

   Building an emergency fund for unexpected expenses can reduce financial stress. Experts at the Consumer Financial Protection Bureau (CFPB) recommend saving three to six months' worth of living expenses (CFPB)

5. **Debt Management:**

   Addressing and managing debt together is crucial. The Federal Trade Commission (FTC) offers resources on debt management and credit counseling (FTC).

6. **Financial Independence and Autonomy:**

   While sharing financial goals, also maintain some financial independence. The American Psychological Association (APA) highlights the importance of maintaining personal financial autonomy (APA, 2018).

7. **Savings and Investments:**

   Educate yourselves about savings accounts, investments, and retirement planning. Resources from websites like The Balance offer guidance on savings and investments (The Balance).

8. **Regular Financial Check-Ins:**

   Schedule regular financial discussions to track progress and address any concerns. Forbes suggests monthly money meetings for couples (Forbes).

9. **Plan for Major Expenses:**

   Planning for significant life events such as buying a home or starting a family is essential. Harvard Business Review offers insights into financial planning for couples (HBR, 2017).

10. **Seek Professional Advice When Necessary:**

    Don't hesitate to consult financial professionals like financial advisors or marriage counselors when facing complex financial issues. The National Association of Personal

"Honour the Lord with thy substance, and with the firstfruits of all thine increase: So shall thy barns be filled with plenty, and thy presses shall burst out with new wine."
Proverbs 3:9-10 KJV

"Anyone who does not provide for their relatives, and especially for their own household, has denied the faith and is worse than an unbeliever."
1 Timothy 5:8 NIV

Positive Affirmation

With God, all things are possible.

~ Matthew 19:26

This affirmation reinforces the idea that success and opportunities are achievable through your faith in God.

10 Ways to Address the Negative Effects of Finances on a Relationship:

1. **Open Communication**:

   Regularly engage in open and honest conversations about your financial situation, goals, and concerns. Establish an environment where both partners feel comfortable discussing money matters.

2. **Set Financial Goals Together:**

   Collaboratively define financial goals and priorities as a couple. Whether it's saving for a vacation, buying a home, or planning for retirement, working together towards common objectives fosters financial harmony.

3. **Create a Joint Budget:**

   Develop a shared budget that outlines how you'll manage expenses and allocate resources. Ensure that both partners have input and agree on the budget and be prepared to make compromises.

4. **Financial Accountability:**

   Assign responsibilities for financial tasks, such as bill payment, tracking expenses, and investments. When both partners play an active role in managing finances, it reduces the risk of misunderstandings and disputes.

5. **Emergency Fund:**

   Maintain an emergency fund to cover unexpected expenses, like medical bills or car repairs. This can alleviate financial stress and prevent disputes when unforeseen costs arise.

6. **Individual Financial Autonomy:**

   While collaboration is crucial, it's also important to respect each other's financial autonomy. Set aside a portion of the budget for personal discretionary spending, allowing both partners to make financial decisions without interference.

7. **Professional Guidance:**

   Consider seeking advice from a financial advisor or counselor who specializes in relationship and financial issues. They can provide expert insights and mediate discussions on complex financial matters.

8. **Debt Management:**

   If you have debts, create a plan to manage and pay them off. Discuss your approach to debt repayment and work together to reduce debt-related stress.

9. **Regular Reviews:**

   Schedule regular financial check-ins to review your budget, progress toward financial goals, and address any concerns or changes in circumstances. This ensures that you stay aligned over time.

10. **Mutual Support:**

    Be understanding and supportive of each other's financial challenges and aspirations. Encourage one another and provide emotional support during financial setbacks and accomplishments.

It is always good to remember that financial challenges are common in relationships, but they can be managed effectively with open communication, collaboration, and mutual respect. It's important to approach financial issues as a team and seek solutions that work for both partners.

Positive Affirmation

**I will focus my thoughts on my family
and myself deserving of happiness,
abundance, and fulfillment in our lives.**

10 Ways to Mitigate the Negative Effects of Finances on a Relationship

1. **Open Communication**:

   Regularly engage in open and honest conversations about your financial situation, goals, and concerns. Establish an environment where both partners feel comfortable discussing money matters.

2. **Set Financial Goals Together**:

   Collaboratively define financial goals and priorities as a couple. Whether it's saving for a vacation, buying a home, or planning for retirement, working together towards common objectives fosters financial harmony.

3. **Create a Joint Budget**:

   Develop a shared budget that outlines how you'll manage expenses and allocate resources. Ensure that both partners have input and agree on the budget, and be prepared to make compromises.

4. **Financial Accountability**:

   Assign responsibilities for financial tasks, such as bill payment, tracking expenses, and investments. When both partners play an active role in managing finances, it reduces the risk of misunderstandings and disputes.

5. **Emergency Fund**:

   Maintain an emergency fund to cover unexpected expenses, like medical bills or car repairs. This can alleviate financial stress and prevent disputes when unforeseen costs arise.

6. **Individual Financial Autonomy**:

   While collaboration is crucial, it's also important to respect each other's financial autonomy. Set aside a portion of the budget for personal discretionary spending, allowing both partners to make financial decisions without interference.

7. **Professional Guidance**:

   Consider seeking advice from a financial advisor or counselor who specializes in relationship and financial issues. They can provide expert insights and mediate discussions on complex financial matters.

8. **Debt Management**:

   If you have debts, create a plan to manage and pay them off. Discuss your approach to debt repayment and work together to reduce debt-related stress.

9. **Regular Reviews**:

   Schedule regular financial check-ins to review your budget, and progress toward financial goals, and address any concerns or changes in circumstances. This ensures that you stay aligned over time.

10. **Mutual Support**:

    Be understanding and supportive of each other's financial challenges and aspirations. Encourage one another and provide emotional support during financial setbacks and accomplishments.

Financial challenges are common in relationships, but they can be managed effectively with open communication, collaboration, and mutual respect. It's important to approach financial issues as a team and seek solutions that work for both partners

Positive Affirmation

**I take every thought captive
to the obedience of Christ.**

~ II Corinthians 10:5

This affirmation encourages you to maintain control over your thoughts and emotions, aligning them with Christ's teachings.

10 Important Facts Regarding Intimacy in a Relationship

1. **Open and Honest Communication**

   Effective communication is key to intimacy. In "Emotional Intimacy: The Art of Talking and Listening" by John Amodeo (Psychology Today, 2019), open and honest communication fosters emotional connection.

2. **Trust**

   Trust is the foundation of intimacy. Dr. John Gottman's research on relationships, as mentioned in "The Science of Trust" (Gottman, J., 2011), underscores the importance of trust in building emotional intimacy.

3. **Emotional Connection**

   Emotional intimacy involves connecting on a deep emotional level. The American Psychological Association (APA) emphasizes the role of emotional connection in intimacy (APA, 2019).

4. **Physical Intimacy**

   Physical closeness, including sexual intimacy, is an important aspect of many romantic relationships. (Mayo Clinic, 2021).

5. **Respect for Boundaries**

   Respecting each other's boundaries and consent is crucial. This principle is emphasized in numerous relationship advice articles, such as "Healthy

Relationships" by Loveisrespect.org (Loveisrespect.org, n.d.).

6. **Vulnerability**

Being open and vulnerable with your partner can deepen intimacy. Brene Brown addresses this work on vulnerability, including her book "Daring Greatly" (Brown, B., 2012), which explores the importance of vulnerability in relationships.

7. **Quality Time Together**

Spending quality time together strengthens the emotional connection. The article "The Importance of Quality Time" by PositivePsychology.com (PositivePsychology.com, 2020) discusses the value of quality time in relationships.

8. **Variety and Adventure**

Trying new experiences together can reignite intimacy. The New York Times highlights the role of novelty in maintaining intimacy in long-term relationships (New York Times, 2018).

9. **Affection and Appreciation**

Regularly showing affection and appreciation reinforces emotional bonds. The Gottman Institute, in its article "The Magic Relationship Ratio" Emphasizes the importance of Positive Interactions. (Gottman, J., 2015),

10. **Intimacy Education**

Continuously learning about intimacy and each other's needs is essential. Resources like the American

Association of Sexuality Educators, Counselors, and Therapists (AASECT) offer information and professionals who can help (AASECT).

"Let him kiss me with the kisses of his mouth: for thy love is better than wine."   *~ Song of Solomon 1:2 KJV*

Positive Affirmation

I am deserving of happiness, abundance, and fulfillment in my life.

This affirmation reinforces your self-worth and reminds you that you deserve to lead a happy, abundant, and fulfilling life.

10 Positive Things Singles Can Do to Enjoy and Enrich Their Lives.

1. Travel and Explore:

Embark on solo adventures to new destinations. Traveling alone allows you to discover new cultures and experiences at your own pace. "The Solo Travel Handbook" by Lonely Planet (2018).

2. Pursue Hobbies:

Dedicate time to hobbies and passions you love. Engaging in activities you're passionate about can bring joy and fulfillment.

3. Socialize and Meet New People:

Attend social events, clubs, or gatherings to expand your social circle. The article "The Art of Mingling" by Jeanne Martinet (2006) offers tips on networking and socializing.

4. Volunteer:

Give back to the community by volunteering for a cause you care about. Volunteering can be a fulfilling way to spend your time. "The Volunteer's Guide to Helping Children and Teens" by Ron Fry (2001).

5. Exercise and Stay Active:

Engage in physical activities that you enjoy, whether it's hiking, dancing, or practicing yoga. Regular exercise is known for its physical and mental health benefits. "The Joy of Movement" by Kelly McGonigal (2020).

6. **Learn Something New:**

   Enroll in courses or workshops to acquire new skills or knowledge. Lifelong learning can be a source of personal growth and enjoyment. Source: Local educational institutions, online courses, and libraries.

7. **Read and Explore Literature:**

   Dive into books, magazines, or audiobooks. Reading allows you to escape into different worlds and gain new perspectives. Source: Various literary works, libraries, and bookstores.

8. **Attend Cultural Events:**

   Attending concerts, theater productions, art exhibitions, and other cultural events. Exploring the arts can be intellectually stimulating and enjoyable.

9. **Cook and Explore Culinary Skills:**

   Experiment with cooking and try new recipes or cuisines. Cooking can be a creative and delicious endeavor. Source: Cooking websites, cookbooks, and culinary classes.

10. **Relax and Practice Self-Care:**

    Take time to relax, meditate, practice mindfulness, or treat yourself to a spa day. Self-care is essential for mental and emotional well-being. "The Self-Care Solution" by Julie Burton (2016).

"But I would have you without carefulness. He that is unmarried careth for the things that belong to the Lord, how he may please the Lord: But he that is married careth for the things that are of the world, how he may

please his wife. There is a difference also between a wife and a virgin. The unmarried woman careth for the things of the Lord, that she may be holy both in body and in spirit: but she that is married careth for the things of the world, how she may please her husband. And this I speak for your own profit; not that I may cast a snare upon you, but for that which is comely, and that ye may attend upon the Lord without distraction."   ~ *1 Corinthians 7:32-35 KJV*

Positive Affirmation

I am fearfully and wonderfully made.

~ Psalm 139:14

This affirmation reminds you of your inherent worthiness and the happiness, abundance, and fulfillment that comes from God's creation.

10 Lessons on the Importance
of Healthy Friendships

1. **"Friendship Enriches Life":**

   Friendships add depth and richness to life, providing companionship and emotional support.

   Aristotle's "Nicomachean Ethics," translated by Terence Irwin (1999).

2. **"Shared Experiences Build Bonds":**

   Experiencing life together creates lasting connections and shared memories that strengthen friendships.

   Source: Dan Buettner's "The Blue Zones: Lessons for Living Longer From the People Who've Lived the Longest" (2009). ISBN

3. **"Friendship Nurtures Mental Health":**

   Friends play a crucial role in providing emotional support and reducing stress and loneliness.

   Source: Hara Estroff Marano's "A Nation of Wimps: The High Cost of Invasive Parenting" (2008). ISBN

4. **"Trust and Loyalty Are Cornerstones":**

   Trust and loyalty are essential aspects of any meaningful friendship.

   Stephen R. Covey's "The Speed of Trust: The One Thing That Changes Everything" (2006).

5. **"Empathy and Understanding Matter":**

The ability to empathize and understand a friend's perspective fosters deeper connections.

Brené Brown's "Daring Greatly: How the Courage to Be Vulnerable Transforms the Way We Live, Love, Parent, and Lead" (2012).

6. **"Quality Over Quantity":**

It's the quality of friendships, not the quantity, that truly matters in life. Shasta Nelson's "Frientimacy: How to Deepen Friendships for Lifelong Health and Happiness" (2016).

7. **"Forgiveness and Conflict Resolution":**

Learning to forgive and resolve conflicts strengthens the longevity of friendships.

Robert D. Enright's "The Forgiving Life: A Pathway to Overcoming Resentment and Creating a Legacy of Love" (2012).

8. **"Diverse Friendships Broaden Perspectives":**

Having friends from different backgrounds can lead to personal growth and expanded horizons.

Tania Israel's "Beyond Your Bubble: How to Connect Across the Political Divide, Skills and Strategies for Conversations That Work" (2020).

9. **"Supportive Friends Encourage Growth":**

Friends who encourage personal development and self-improvement are invaluable.

Carol S. Dweck's "Mindset: The New Psychology of Success" (2006).

10. "Friendships Are Worth Investing In":

Maintaining friendships requires effort and time, but the rewards are immeasurable.

Jane Isay's "Walking on Eggshells: Navigating the Delicate Relationship Between Adult Children and Parents" (2008).

"A man that hath friends must shew himself friendly: and there is a friend that sticketh closer than a brother."
Proverbs 18:24 KJV

10 Things a Person Should Work on Themselves Before Getting into a Relationship

1. **Self-Awareness:**

   Understanding one's values, needs, and emotions is crucial. Self-awareness contributes to healthy relationships. Source: "Emotional Intelligence" by Daniel Goleman (1995).

2. **Self-Esteem:**

   Building self-esteem and self-worth can enhance one's confidence and resilience in relationships. Source: "The Six Pillars of Self-Esteem" by Nathaniel Branden (1994).

3. **Independence:**

   Foster self-sufficiency and independence in various aspects of life, including finances, so that you don't rely solely on a partner. Source: "Codependent No More" by Melody Beattie (1986).

4. **Communication Skills:**

   Developing effective communication skills can prevent misunderstandings and conflicts in relationships. Source: "Nonviolent Communication" by Marshall B. Rosenberg (1999).

5. **Boundaries:**

Establish and maintain healthy boundaries to protect your emotional and physical well-being. Source: "Boundaries: When to Say Yes, How to Say No to Take Control of Your Life" by Dr. Henry Cloud and Dr. John Townsend (1992).

6. **Emotional Resilience:**

Strengthen emotional resilience to cope with life's challenges and setbacks, ensuring you can support yourself and your partner. Source: "The Resilience Factor" by Karen Reivich and Andrew Shatté (2003).

7. **Self-Care:**

Prioritize self-care practices, such as physical fitness and mental well-being, to ensure you can give your best in a relationship. Source: "The Self-Care Solution" by Julie Burton (2016).

8. **Life Goals:**

Define and work toward personal and career goals, ensuring you have a sense of direction and purpose. Source: "The 7 Habits of Highly Effective People" by Stephen R. Covey (1989).

9. **Past Relationship Reflection:**

Reflect on past relationships and learn from them to avoid repeating unhealthy patterns. Source: "Getting Past Your Breakup" by Susan J. Elliott (2009).

10. Independence of Happiness:

Cultivate personal happiness and fulfillment independently, so you're not reliant on a relationship for your well-being. Source: "The Happiness Project" by Gretchen Rubin (2009)

"For if any be a hearer of the word and not a doer, he is like unto a man beholding his natural face in a glass: For he beholdeth himself, and goeth his way, and straightway forgetteth what manner of man he was." ~ James 1:23-24

10 Things That Can Happen in a Relationship Where The Couple is Unequally Yoked (Positive)

Being "unequally yoked" typically refers to a relationship where partners have significant differences in their beliefs, values, or life goals. While such relationships can pose challenges, they can still thrive if both individuals are willing to work through their differences and find common ground.

While it is important to note that in most cases being unequally yoked will lead to an unhealthy relationship some couples may have gotten together while one or both were unsaved. Does this automatically mean the marriage will not work?

10 ways the relationship between them can work out:

1. Growth and Learning:

Being in a relationship where partners have differing beliefs or values can be an opportunity for both individuals to grow and learn. They are exposed to different perspectives and are often encouraged to reevaluate their own beliefs and values. This can lead to personal growth as they expand their horizons and deepen their understanding of the world.

2. Broadened Horizons:

Couples with varying beliefs or interests can introduce each other to new experiences and ideas. This exposure can be enriching, allowing each partner to learn about different cultures, traditions, and ways of thinking. It can lead to a more open-minded and well-rounded worldview.

3. **Enhanced Communication Skills:**

   Unequally yoked couples often face challenges when discussing their differences. To maintain a healthy relationship, they must develop strong communication skills. This includes active listening, empathy, and the ability to express their thoughts and feelings effectively.

4. **Increased Tolerance and Acceptance:**

   Over time, couples in such relationships may develop a greater tolerance for differing viewpoints and a deeper appreciation for diversity. This can extend beyond the relationship to positively impact how they interact with others in various aspects of life.

5. **Creative Problem Solving:**

   Navigating differences in beliefs or values can lead to creative problem-solving. Couples find innovative ways to accommodate each other's needs and find compromises that work for both. This can enhance their ability to tackle challenges together.

6. **Deeper Emotional Connection:**

   Successfully working through differences can lead to a deeper emotional connection. Partners may find that they have a profound understanding of each other's struggles and triumphs, which can create a strong bond built on support and empathy.

7. **Stronger Bond:**

The shared commitment to making the relationship work can lead to a stronger bond. Couples in unequally yoked relationships often face external challenges and societal judgments, which can draw them closer together as they face these obstacles as a team.

8. **Mutual Respect:**

Learning to navigate differences fosters a deep sense of respect for each other's unique qualities. Recognizing and accepting each other's individuality is a fundamental component of a successful unequally yoked relationship.

9. **Personal Fulfillment:**

While navigating differences, individuals may have the opportunity to pursue their own passions and beliefs. This personal fulfillment can lead to happiness and contentment, which, in turn, can positively impact the relationship.

10. **Modeling Diversity:**

Unequally yoked relationships can serve as models for diversity and inclusivity. They show that love and respect can transcend differences, setting an example for others in how to navigate and celebrate diversity in all its forms.

It's important to remember that while these positive aspects can be present in unequally yoked relationships, success often depends on open communication, mutual respect, and a willingness to work through differences. However, it's equally important to recognize when differences become insurmountable or when they negatively impact the well-being of one or both partners. Seeking guidance from a relationship counselor or therapist can be invaluable in helping couples navigate the unique challenges of their relationship and make informed decisions about its future.

10 Things That Can Happen in a Relationship Where The Couple is Unequally Yoked (Negative)

1. Conflict and Tension:

Differing beliefs and values can lead to frequent conflicts and heightened tension in the relationship. These arguments may revolve around topics like religion, politics, or fundamental life choices, causing emotional strain for both partners.

2. Communication Breakdown:

The presence of stark differences in beliefs can lead to misunderstandings and breakdowns in communication. Partners may struggle to express their thoughts and feelings effectively, making it difficult to resolve conflicts or address concerns.

3. Lack of Shared Goals:

Partners with conflicting beliefs may struggle to establish common goals for their future. These differences can lead to a lack of shared aspirations and a sense of being on separate life paths, which can strain the relationship.

4. Emotional Stress:

Unequally yoked relationships can be emotionally stressful. Partners may constantly worry about how their differences may impact the future of the relationship, causing anxiety, emotional strain, and uncertainty

5. Social Isolation:

Divergent interests and values can lead to social isolation as couples may find it challenging to engage in shared activities or socialize together. This can result in feelings of loneliness and detachment from each other's social circles.

6. Religious or Cultural Conflicts:

In cases where differences in religious or cultural backgrounds are significant, conflicts may arise with family members and within the community. These conflicts can add additional stress to the relationship as partners navigate the pressures and expectations from external sources.

7. Pressure to Change:

One or both partners may feel pressured to change their beliefs or values to align with the others. This pressure can lead to feelings of resentment, inauthenticity, and a loss of individual identity.

8. Lack of Support:

Unequally yoked couples may struggle to find support and understanding from their friends and family. Loved ones may not be accepting of the relationship, which can result in feelings of isolation and strain within the relationship.

9. Unresolved Differences:

Despite efforts to compromise, some differences may prove insurmountable. Unequally yoked couples may find certain issues to remain unresolved, causing ongoing discontent and frustration.

10. Dissatisfaction and Unhappiness:

Over time, the accumulation of negative effects can result in overall dissatisfaction and unhappiness in the relationship. Partners may feel unfulfilled and question the long-term viability of the relationship, which can lead to a sense of disillusionment.

It's essential to understand that these negative effects are not inevitable in every unequally yoked relationship. Many couples successfully navigate their differences by engaging in open and honest communication, practicing compromise, and maintaining a shared commitment to the relationship's well-being. In some cases, seeking guidance from a relationship counselor or therapist can be beneficial in helping couples manage and address these challenges. Ultimately, the success of such a relationship depends on the individuals involved and their willingness to work together to overcome these potential obstacles.

Positive Affirmation

**I am grateful for the present moment
and excited for the future.**

This affirmation encourages a balance between
appreciating the present and looking forward to the
future. Gratitude and excitement can motivate and
inspire you.

10 Steps to Getting Along with Friends, Family, and Others

1. **Effective Communication:**

   Communicate openly and honestly. As highlighted in the book "Crucial Conversations" by Al Switzler, Joseph Grenny, and Ron McMillan (2002), effective communication is crucial for resolving conflicts and building relationships.

2. **Empathy and Active Listening:**

   Practice empathy and active listening to understand others better. The article "The Art of Empathetic Listening" by Psychology Today (Psychology Today, 2015) emphasizes the importance of active listening.

3. **Respect Boundaries:**

   Respect personal boundaries and preferences. "Boundaries: When to Say Yes, How to Say No to Take Control of Your Life" by Dr. Henry Cloud and Dr. John Townsend (1992) explores the concept of boundaries in relationships.

4. **Conflict Resolution Skills:**

   Learn conflict resolution skills. "Difficult Conversations: How to Discuss What Matters Most" by Douglas Stone, Bruce Patton, and Sheila Heen (1999) provides insights into addressing challenging conversations.

5. **Forgiveness:**

   Practice forgiveness and let go of grudges. The Mayo Clinic's article "Forgiveness: Letting Go of Grudges and Bitterness" (Mayo Clinic, 2018) discusses the health benefits of forgiveness.

6. **Shared Activities:**

   Engage in shared activities and hobbies. The Psychology Today article "The Benefits of Having Hobbies" (Psychology Today, 2019) discusses the positive impact of shared interests.

7. **Positive Communication:**

   Use positive communication techniques. The article "Positive Communication: 6 Simple Tips for Success" by (Help Guide, 2021) offers guidance on positive communication.

8. **Express Gratitude:**

   Express gratitude and appreciation. The Greater Good Science Center's article "How to Cultivate Gratitude" (Greater Good Magazine, 2019) discusses the benefits of gratitude in relationships.

9. **Boundaries and Self-Care:**

   Set and maintain boundaries to prioritize self-care. "Boundaries: Where You End, and I Begin" by Anne Katherine (1991) explores the importance of boundaries in relationships.

10. Seeking Professional Help:

When necessary, consider seeking professional help, such as family therapy or counseling, to address complex relationship dynamics. The American Association for Marriage and Family Therapy (AAMFT) offers resources and a directory of therapists (AAMFT).

"Let love be without dissimulation. Abhor that which is evil; cleave to that which is good."   *Romans 12:9 KJV*

Positive Affirmation

**This is the day the Lord has made;
I will rejoice and be glad in it.**

~ Psalm 118:24

This affirmation emphasizes gratitude for the present moment and excitement for the future, acknowledging that each day is a gift from God.

10 Negative Things that Should Not be Heard in a Healthy Relationship:

1. **Insults and Name-Calling:**

   Avoid using hurtful language or derogatory names when communicating with your partner. These words can cause emotional harm and damage self-esteem.

2. **Threats or Ultimatums:**

   Making threats or issuing ultimatums can create a hostile environment and damage trust. Healthy communication focuses on understanding and compromise.

3. **Blame and Accusations:**

   Constantly blaming your partner for issues or accusing them without evidence can lead to defensiveness and resentment.

4. **Comparisons to Others:**

   Comparing your partner unfavorably to others, especially in terms of appearance or achievements, can be hurtful and damaging to self-esteem.

5. **Bringing Up Past Mistakes:**

   Continuously bringing up past mistakes or grievances can prevent healing and forgiveness. Healthy relationships involve moving forward.

6. **Negative Criticism:**

   While constructive feedback is valuable, constant negative criticism without offering solutions can erode self-confidence and hinder personal growth.

7. **Silent Treatment:**

   Ignoring or giving your partner the silent treatment can create emotional distance and make conflict resolution difficult.

8. **Sarcasm and Mockery:**

   Using sarcasm or mockery can be hurtful and dismissive, undermining open and honest communication.

9. **Guilt-Tripping:**

   Attempting to manipulate your partner by making them feel guilty is unhealthy and can lead to emotional manipulation.

10. **Invalidating Feelings:**

    Dismissing or invalidating your partner's feelings or experiences can make them feel unheard and unvalued.

"A soft answer turneth away wrath: but grievous words stir up anger." ~ *Proverbs 15:1 KJV*

10 Signs of an Unhealthy Relationship

1. **Lack of Communication:**

   In an unhealthy relationship, communication may be minimal or non-existent. Partners may avoid discussing their feelings or concerns, leading to misunderstandings and pent-up emotions.

2. **Constant Criticism:**

   Criticism, belittling, or demeaning behavior is a sign of an unhealthy relationship. Partners should support and uplift each other, not constantly criticize, or put each other down.

3. **Control and Manipulation:**

   One partner may exert control and manipulate the other's decisions, actions, or freedom. Healthy relationships are based on mutual respect and autonomy.

4. **Isolation:**

   An unhealthy relationship may involve one partner isolating the other from friends and family, making it difficult to maintain external connections.

5. **Lack of Trust:**

   Trust is essential in any relationship. If trust is consistently broken, with one partner being dishonest or suspicious, it can lead to an unhealthy dynamic.

6. **Emotional or Physical Abuse:**

   Any form of abuse, whether emotional, physical, or sexual, is a clear sign of an unhealthy relationship and should not be tolerated.

7. **Constant Arguments:**

   While disagreements are normal, a constant state of conflict, hostility, or shouting matches is unhealthy and emotionally draining.

8. **Dependence:**

   When one partner becomes overly dependent on the other for emotional, financial, or other needs, it can lead to an unhealthy power imbalance.

9. **Stonewalling:**

   Stonewalling is when one partner withdraws from communication and refuses to engage in resolving conflicts. This can lead to unresolved issues and emotional distance.

10. **Lack of Personal Growth:**

    In an unhealthy relationship, personal growth and self-improvement may be discouraged or hindered, preventing individuals from reaching their full potential.

If you recognize any of these signs in your relationship, it's essential to seek help and support, whether through counseling, therapy, or reaching out to a trusted friend or family member. Remember that a healthy relationship should be based on mutual respect, trust, and emotional well-being for both partners.

"Put on therefore, as the elect of God, holy and beloved, bowels of mercies, kindness, humbleness of mind, meekness, longsuffering; Forbearing one another, and forgiving one another, if any man have a quarrel against any: even as Christ forgave you, so also do ye. And above all these things put on charity [love], which is the bond of perfectness."
~ Colossians 3:12-14 KJV

Positive Affirmation

My positivity shines, inspiring and uplifting those around me.

This affirmation highlights the impact your positivity can have on others. It encourages you to be a source of inspiration and support to those in your life.

10 Ways to Reconcile After a Divorce

Many couples realize after divorcing that they actually miss their spouse and realize the problems they had were not as serious as they thought.

1. **Open and Honest Communication:**

   Reconciliation begins with honest and open communication. Both partners should be willing to talk about their feelings and experiences during the divorce. Discuss what went wrong in the marriage, why you want to reconcile, and what changes need to be made for the relationship to succeed. Effective communication is the cornerstone of any successful reconciliation effort.

2. **Counseling or Therapy:**

   Seeking professional help is often a wise step in the reconciliation process. Couples therapy or counseling provides a safe space for discussing issues, learning effective communication strategies, and gaining insights from a trained therapist. A neutral third party can help mediate discussions and guide the process of rebuilding the relationship.

3. **Time and Space:**

   Taking some time apart can be beneficial. It allows both individuals to reflect on the relationship, their own contributions to its difficulties, and their feelings about the divorce. This separation should not be indefinite but rather a period for introspection, during which you can assess whether reconciliation is a genuine desire and a healthy choice.

4. **Mutual Understanding and Forgiveness:**

Reconciliation requires mutual understanding and forgiveness. Both partners need to comprehend each other's perspectives and be willing to forgive past mistakes and hurts. This process can be emotionally challenging, but it is essential for moving forward with a clean slate.

5. **Addressing Root Issues:**

To prevent the same problems from resurfacing, it's crucial to identify and address the root causes of the divorce. This may involve delving into issues such as communication breakdowns, trust issues, financial problems, or unresolved conflicts. Developing strategies to overcome these issues is essential for a successful reconciliation.

6. **Commitment to Change:**

Words alone are not enough. Both partners must commit to making real changes. Whether it's improving communication, managing conflicts better, or addressing personal issues that contributed to the divorce, taking action is crucial. A commitment to personal growth and relationship improvement is necessary.

7. **Rebuilding Trust:**

Trust, once eroded, can be difficult to rebuild. Re-establishing trust takes time and consistent effort. Both partners must demonstrate trustworthiness and reliability. Building trust involves keeping promises, being transparent, and showing through actions that you can be relied upon.

8. **Shared Goals and Values:**

   Ensure that you both share common goals, values, and a vision for the future. This shared foundation is vital for the long-term success of the relationship. Establishing a strong mutual understanding of what you both want out of the relationship can help align your efforts towards reconciliation.

9. **Reconnecting Emotionally and Physically:**

   Rekindling emotional and physical intimacy is essential. Spend quality time together, go on dates, and engage in activities that you both enjoy. Rebuilding the emotional connection might require shared experiences and open conversations about your feelings.

10. **Legal Steps:**

   If you are considering reconciliation after a divorce, consult with a legal professional to understand the legal implications and requirements in your jurisdiction. In some cases, reconciliation may involve remarrying, and you need to be aware of the legal process and requirements for doing so.

Reconciliation after a divorce is a deeply personal and often challenging journey. It's essential to approach it with realistic expectations and to seek guidance from professionals when needed. Ultimately, the success of reconciliation depends on the willingness of both partners to work together, communicate openly, and make the necessary changes to rebuild the relationship.

Positive Affirmation

Let your light so shine before men, that they may see your good works and glorify your Father in heaven.

~ Matthew 5:16

This affirmation encourages you to radiate positivity, inspiring and uplifting those around you for God's glory and to learn to appreciate every minute of every day.

10 Romantic Poems

1. **"Love's Philosophy" by Percy Bysshe Shelley**
"Percy Bysshe Shelley: The Major Works" edited by Zachary Leader.

   "The fountains mingle with the river and the rivers with the ocean, The winds of heaven mix forever With a sweet emotion; Nothing in the world is single; All things by a law divine In one spirit meet and mingle. Why not I with thine?—"

2. **"How Do I Love Thee?" by Elizabeth Barrett Browning**
"Sonnets from the Portuguese" by Elizabeth Barrett Browning.

   "How do I love thee? Let me count the ways. I love thee to the depth and breadth and height My soul can reach when feeling out of sight for the ends of being and ideal grace".

3. **"A Red, Red Rose" by Robert Burns**
"Robert Burns: Poems and Songs" edited by Robert P. Irvine.

   "O, my luve's like a red, red rose, That's newly sprung in June: O, my luve's like the melodie, That's sweetly play'd in tune."

4. **"I Carry Your Heart with Me" by E.E. Cummings**
"Complete Poems, 1904-1962" by E.E. Cummings.
   "I carry your heart with me (I carry it in my heart) I am never without it (anywhere I go you go, my dear; and whatever is done by only me is your doing, my darling)"

5. **"Sonnet 18: Shall I Compare Thee to a Summer's Day?" by William Shakespeare**
"Shakespeare's Sonnets" edited by Katherine Duncan-Jones.

"Shall I compare thee to a summer's day? Thou art more lovely and more temperate: Rough winds do shake the darling buds of May,"

6. **"Annabel Lee" by Edgar Allan Poe**
"Edgar Allan Poe: Complete Tales and Poems" by Edgar Allan Poe.

"But we loved with a love that was more than love— I and my Annabel Lee— With a love that the wingèd seraphs of Heaven Coveted her and me".

7. **"Love Is More Thicker Than Forget" by e.e. Cummings**
Complete Poems, 1904-1962" by E.E. Cummings.

"Love is more thicker than forget more thinner than recall more seldom than a wave is wet more frequent than to fail"

8. **"The Good-Morrow" by John Donne**
"Selected Poems" by John Donne. ISBN: 978-0140422093.
"For love, all love of other sights controls, And makes one little room an everywhere. Let sea-discoverers to new worlds have gone;"

9. **"Love's Philosophy" by Lord Byron**
"Lord Byron: The Major Works" edited by Jerome J. McGann.

"The fountains mingle with the river And the rivers with the ocean, The winds of heaven mix forever With a sweet emotion;"

10. **"The Passionate Shepherd to His Love" by Christopher Marlowe**

   "The Complete Works of Christopher Marlowe" edited by Roma Gill.

   "Come live with me and be my love, and we will all the pleasures prove That valleys, groves, hills, and fields, Woods or steepy mountain yields."

"The king's daughter is all glorious within: her clothing is of wrought gold. She shall be brought unto the king in raiment of needlework: the virgins her companions that follow her shall be brought unto thee. With gladness and rejoicing shall they be brought: they shall enter into the king's palace."
~ Psalms 45:13-15 KJV

Positive Affirmation

I express gratitude for the present moment and enthusiasm for what the future holds.

This affirmation underscores the value of personal growth and learning from life's experiences. It encourages you to view every experience, whether positive or negative, as an opportunity for growth.

10 Negative Things that Should Never Be Said or Done in a Marriage:

1. **Divorce Threats:**

   Avoid making threats of divorce or separation during arguments. Such statements can undermine the stability of the marriage.

2. **Insults and Name-Calling:**

   Using hurtful language or derogatory names toward your spouse can cause emotional harm and damage the marital bond.

3. **Personal Attacks:**

   Avoid personal attacks on your spouse's character, appearance, or abilities. These attacks can be deeply hurtful and erode self-esteem.

4. **Bringing Up Past Mistakes:**

   Continuously bringing up past mistakes or grievances can hinder forgiveness and healing in the relationship.

5. **Comparisons to Others:**

   Comparing your spouse unfavorably to others, whether it's about appearance, achievements, or behavior, can be hurtful and detrimental to self-esteem.

6. **Blame and Accusations:**

Constantly blaming your spouse for issues or accusing them without evidence can lead to defensiveness and resentment.

7. **Negative Criticism:**

While constructive feedback is important, constant negative criticism without offering solutions can damage self-confidence and hinder personal growth.

8. **Silent Treatment:**

Ignoring or giving your spouse silent treatment can create emotional distance and hinder effective communication.

9. **Sarcasm and Mockery:**

Using sarcasm or mockery can be hurtful and dismissive, making it difficult to maintain respectful communication.

10. **Guilt-Tripping:**

Attempting to manipulate your spouse by making them feel guilty is unhealthy and can lead to emotional manipulation within the marriage.

"A soft answer turneth away wrath: but grievous words stir up anger." ~ *Proverbs 15:1 KJV*

10 Ways to Make Up After an Argument or Disagreement in a Relationship

1. **"Apologize Sincerely"**

   Offer a genuine apology, acknowledging your part in the disagreement. Chapman, G. (1995). "The Five Love Languages: How to Express Heartfelt Commitment to Your Mate."

2. **"Active Listening"**

   Practice active listening to understand your partner's perspective and validate their feelings. Covey, S. R. (1989). "The 7 Habits of Highly Effective People."

3. **"Take a Break"**

   Sometimes, a short break from the argument can allow both parties to cool down and think more rationally. Gottman, J., & Silver, N. (2015). "The Seven Principles for Making Marriage Work."

4. **"Use 'I' Statements"**

   Express your feelings using "I" statements to avoid blaming your partner. Patterson, K., Grenny, J., McMillan, R., & Switzler, A. (2002). "Crucial Conversations: Tools for Talking When Stakes Are High."

5. **"Find Common Ground"**

   Identify areas of agreement and common goals to reestablish a sense of unity. Heitler, S. M. (2009). "The Power of Two Workbook: Communication Skills for a Strong & Loving Marriage.

6. **"Empathize and Validate"**

Show empathy and validate your partner's emotions, even if you don't agree with their perspective. Brown, B. (2012). "Daring Greatly: How the Courage to Be Vulnerable Transforms the Way We Live, Love, Parent, and Lead."

7. **"Forgive and Let Go"**

Practice forgiveness and let go of grudges to move forward positively. Enright, R. D. (2001). "Forgiveness Is a Choice: A Step-by-Step Process for Resolving Anger and Restoring Hope."

8. **"Set Boundaries for Future Disagreements"**

Discuss how you can handle disagreements constructively in the future. Cloud, H., & Townsend, J. (1992). "Boundaries: When to Say Yes, How to Say No to Take Control of Your Life."

9. **"Express Love and Affection"**

Reconnect emotionally by expressing love and affection toward each other. Chapman, G. (2015)."The 5 Love Languages: The Secret to Love that Lasts."

10. **"Seek Professional Help If Needed"**

If Disagreements persist, consider couples counseling or therapy. Source: Gottman, J., & Gottman, J. S. (2015). "The Seven Principles for Making Marriage Work."

"Wherefore, my beloved brethren, let every man be swift to hear, slow to speak, slow to wrath." ~ James 1:19 KJV

10 Things a Woman Wants to Hear from a Man

What a woman wants to hear from a man can vary depending on her individual preferences and the stage of the relationship.

1. "I love you." This simple phrase can mean a lot and reassure her of your feelings.

2. "You're beautiful." Complimenting her physical appearance can boost her self-esteem and make her feel appreciated.

3. "I'm here for you." Letting her know that you're there to support and listen to her can be very comforting.

4. "You're incredibly smart." Acknowledging her intelligence and accomplishments can be empowering.

5. "I respect you." Respect is crucial in any relationship, and expressing it reinforces the importance you place on her as an individual.

6. "I'm proud of you." Recognizing her achievements and efforts can be very motivating.

7. "You make me a better person." Letting her know that she has a positive impact on your life is a heartwarming sentiment.

8. "I appreciate you." Expressing gratitude for the things she does for you can show that you don't take her for granted.

9. "You're so strong." Recognizing her inner strength and resilience can be empowering.

10. "Let's plan our future together." Discussing plans and goals together can make her feel like you're committed to a long-term relationship.

As with any communication in a relationship, sincerity is crucial. It's important to express these sentiments genuinely and honestly. Additionally, open and honest communication about both partners' needs and feelings is essential for a healthy and thriving relationship.

"Husbands, love your wives, even as Christ also loved the church and gave himself for it." Ephesians 5:25 KJV

10 Things a Man Wants to Hear from a Woman

Just like women, what a man wants to hear from a woman can vary based on individual preferences and the context of their relationship. However, here are 10 generally positive and affirming things that many men may appreciate hearing:

1. "I love you." Men value love and affection just as much as women do, and hearing these words can be deeply meaningful.

2. "You make me feel safe." Letting him know that he provides a sense of security can be reassuring and boost his confidence.

3. "I trust you." Trust is vital in any relationship and expressing it can strengthen the bond between you.

4. "I'm proud of you." Recognizing his achievements and efforts can boost his self-esteem and motivation.

5. "You're handsome." Complimenting his physical appearance can make him feel attractive and desired.

6. "You're so smart." Acknowledging his intelligence and knowledge can be affirming and empowering.

7. "I appreciate you." Expressing gratitude for the things he does for you and the relationship can show that you value his efforts.

8. "You're a great partner." Recognizing his contributions to the relationship can make him feel appreciated.

9. "I believe in you." Showing confidence in his abilities and goals can be motivating and encouraging.

10. "Let's plan our future together." Discussing plans and goals as a couple can demonstrate commitment and a desire for a shared future.

"Likewise, ye wives, be in subjection to your own husbands; that, if any obey not the word, they also may without the word be won by the conversation of the wives." ~ *1 Peter 3:1 KJV*

10 Ways To Show Your Friends and Family You Value and Appreciate Them

1. **Express Gratitude Verbally"**

    Tell your loved ones that you appreciate them with words of thanks and affection. "The Psychology of Gratitude" by Robert A. Emmons and Michael E. McCullough (2004).

2. **"Quality Time"**

    Spend quality time with your friends and family, engaging in meaningful activities and conversations. "The Importance of Quality Time" by PositivePsychology.com (2020).

3. **"Acts of Service"**

    Offer to help with tasks or chores to alleviate their burdens. "The 5 Love Languages: How to Express Heartfelt Commitment to Your Mate" by Gary Chapman (1995).

4. **"Thoughtful Gestures"**

    Surprise them with thoughtful gestures, such as handwritten notes or small gifts.

5. **"Listen Actively"**

    Practice active listening when they talk to you, showing that you value their thoughts and feelings.

    "The 7 Habits of Highly Effective People" by Stephen R. Covey (1989).

6. "Celebrate Milestones"

Acknowledge and celebrate their achievements and important life events.

7. "Offer Support in Times of Need"

Be there for them during challenging times, offering emotional and practical support. "The Speed of Trust: The One Thing That Changes Everything" by Stephen R. Covey (2006).

8. "Respect Their Boundaries"

Respect their boundaries and preferences, demonstrating consideration.

"Boundaries: When to Say Yes, How to Say No to Take Control of Your Life" by Dr. Henry Cloud and Dr. John Townsend (1992).

9. "Share Kind Words"

Compliment and speak kindly to your loved ones, boosting their self-esteem.

"The Power of Positive Thinking" by Norman Vincent Peale (1952).

10. "Remember Special Occasions"

Make an effort to remember and acknowledge birthdays, anniversaries, and other special occasions.
"But if anyone does not provide for his relatives, and especially for members of his household, he has denied the faith and is worse than an unbeliever." ~1 Timothy 5:8 ESV

10 Reasons Why Humor is Important in Your Relationships.

1. Enhances Connection

Humor creates a shared sense of joy and laughter, fostering a stronger emotional bond in relationships. Martin, R. A. (2007). "The Psychology of Humor: An Integrative Approach."

2. Stress Reduction

Laughter and humor are natural stress relievers, helping partners navigate the ups and downs of life with greater ease. Berk, L. S., Tan, S. A., Nehlsen-Cannarella, S. L., et al. (1988).
"Humor as an Intervention for Chronic Pain in Oncology Patients." Journal of Psychosocial Oncology, 6(3-4), 43-52.

3. Promotes Positivity

Humor promotes a positive atmosphere, making it easier to resolve conflicts and face challenges together. Averill, J. R. (1973). "Personal Control Over Aversive Stimuli and Its Relationship to Stress." Psychological Bulletin, 80(4), 286-303.

4. Improves Communication

Playful banter and humor can improve communication by breaking down barriers and reducing defensiveness. Holmes, J. (2006). "Sharing a Laugh: Pragmatic Aspects of Humor and Gender in the Workplace." Journal of Pragmatics, 38(1), 26-50.

5. Boosts Creativity

Humor stimulates creative thinking, which can lead to innovative problem-solving and new ideas in the relationship. Isen, A. M., & Daubman, K. A. (1984). "The Influence of Effect on Categorization." Journal of Personality and Social Psychology, 47(6), 1206-1217.

6. Strengthens Resilience

A good sense of humor can help couples bounce back from setbacks and adapt to changes more easily. Ruch, W., & Hofmann, J. (2017). "Fostering humor." In A. C. Parks & S. M. Schueller (Eds.), "The Wiley Handbook of Positive Clinical Psychology" (pp. 383-404).

7. Promotes Playfulness

Playful interactions and humor keep the relationship exciting and prevent it from becoming monotonous. Fisher, T. D., & Exline, J. J. (2002). "Verbal Aggression in Marriage: An Examination of the Problem and a Review of Two Methods of Intervention." Clinical Psychology Review, 22(7), 945-964.

8. Strengthens Social Bonds

Shared laughter in social settings, including relationships, strengthens social bonds and connections. Dunbar, R. I. (2012). "On the Evolutionary Function of Song and Dance." In D. E. Levitin (Ed.), "This Is Your Brain on Music" (pp. 303-314).

9. Increases Attraction

Humor is often seen as an attractive trait, drawing people closer to each other in relationships. Hall, J. A., & Canterberry, M. (2011). "Sexual Selection and Humor in Courtship: A Case for Warmth and Extroversion." Evolutionary Psychology, 9(3), 467-488.

10. Fosters Playful Intimacy:

Humor can create a sense of playful intimacy, enhancing the romantic and sexual aspects of the relationship. El-Burki, I. (2009). "The Use of Humor in Sex Therapy: A Review." Sexual and Relationship Therapy, 24(1), 2-16.

"A merry heart doeth good like a medicine: but a broken spirit drieth the bones." Proverbs 17:22 KJV

Positive Affirmation

**I express gratitude for the present moment and
enthusiasm for what the future holds.**

This affirmation encourages a balanced perspective on
time. It reminds you to be thankful for what you have
now and to maintain enthusiasm and hope for your
future.

10 Positive Affirmations for Healthy Relationships

1. **"I am worthy of love and respect.** "The Gifts of Imperfection" by Brené Brown.

2. **"I communicate openly and honestly with my partner."** Nonviolent Communication" by Marshall B. Rosenberg.

3. **"I am committed to nurturing our emotional connection."** "Hold Me Tight" by Dr. Sue Johnson.

4. **"I practice empathy and understanding in my relationship.** "The Seven Principles for Making Marriage Work" by Dr. John Gottman.

5. **"I choose to let go of past grievances and forgive."**

   "Forgiveness: Letting Go of Grudges and Bitterness" (Mayo Clinic, 2018).

6. **"I am patient and compassionate in times of conflict.** "Crucial Conversations" by Al Switzler, Joseph Grenny, and Ron McMillan.

7. **"I prioritize self-care to bring my best self to the relationship.** "The Self-Care Solution" by Julie Burton.

8. **"I celebrate our love and cherish our moments together."**

9. **"I am open to growth and learning in my relationship."** "The Relationship Cure" by Dr. John Gottman.

10. **"I am grateful for the love and support in my relationship."** "The Happiness Project" by Gretchen Rubin.

"Pleasant words are as an honeycomb, sweet to the soul, and health to the bones." ~ *Proverbs 16:24 KJV*

"Let your speech be alway with grace, seasoned with salt, that ye may know how ye ought to answer every man." ~ *Colossians 4:6 KJV*

10 Positive Affirmations to Help Others Seeking a Healthy Relationship

1. **I am worthy of love and respect.**

   This affirmation reminds you of your inherent worthiness and sets the expectation for a relationship based on love and mutual respect.

2. **I am open to giving and receiving love.**

   Being open to both giving and receiving love creates a balanced and nurturing dynamic in a relationship.

3. **I attract positive, kind-hearted people into my life.**

   Focusing on attracting positive and kind-hearted individuals helps you set the intention for a healthy and supportive partnership.

4. **I am ready for a loving and fulfilling relationship.**

   This affirmation reflects your readiness to welcome a loving and fulfilling relationship into your life.

5. **I trust my instincts and intuition in matters of the heart.**

   Trusting your instincts helps you make wise choices and form connections that are in alignment with your values.

6. **I let go of past relationship baggage and embrace a fresh start.**

   Releasing the baggage from past relationships allows you to approach new relationships with a clean slate and a positive outlook.

7. **I communicate my needs and boundaries with confidence.**

Effective communication is essential for a healthy relationship, and this affirmation empowers you to express yourself with confidence.

8. **I am patient and allow love to unfold naturally.**

Patience is key in building a lasting and meaningful connection, and this affirmation encourages a gradual and authentic process.

9. **I prioritize self-care and self-love.**

Taking care of yourself and loving yourself first sets the foundation for attracting someone who values and appreciates you.

10. **I am grateful for the love and happiness that will come into my life.**

Gratitude can attract more positivity and love, and this affirmation expresses your readiness to welcome happiness into your life.

Repeating these affirmations regularly can help you maintain a positive mindset and attract the healthy relationship you desire. You can say them aloud, write them down, or even create visual reminders to reinforce these positive beliefs in your life.

10 Scriptures on Love from the Bible

1. **1 Corinthians 13:4-7 (NIV):**

   "Love is patient, love is kind. It does not envy, it does not boast, it is not proud. It does not dishonor others, it is not self-seeking, it is not easily angered, it keeps no record of wrongs. Love does not delight in evil but rejoices with the truth. It always protects, always trusts, always hopes, always perseveres."

2. **John 3:16 (NIV):**

   "For God so loved the world that he gave his one and only Son, that whoever believes in him shall not perish but have eternal life."

3. **Ephesians 4:2 (NIV):**

   "Be completely humble and gentle; be patient, bearing with one another in love."

4. **Song of Solomon 8:6 (NIV):**

   "Place me like a seal over your heart, like a seal on your arm; for love is as strong as death, its jealousy unyielding as the grave. It burns like blazing fire, like a mighty flame."

5. **1 John 4:16 (NIV):**

   "So we have come to know and to believe the love that God has for us. God is love, and anyone who abides in love abides in God, and God abides in them."

6. **Romans 13:10 (NIV):**

"Love does no harm to a neighbor. Therefore, love is the fulfillment of the law."

7. **Colossians 3:14 (NIV):**

   "And over all these virtues put on love, which binds them all together in perfect unity."

8. **Proverbs 10:12 (NIV):**

   "Hatred stirs up conflict, but love covers over all wrongs."

9. **1 Peter 4:8 (NIV):**

   "Above all, love each other deeply, because love covers over a multitude of sins."

10. **1 Corinthians 16:14 (NIV):**

    "Do everything in love."

"Set me as a seal upon thine heart, as a seal upon thine arm: for love is strong as death; jealousy is cruel as the grave: the coals thereof are coals of fire, which hath a most vehement flame. Many waters cannot quench love, neither can the floods drown it: if a man would give all the substance of his house for love, it would utterly be contemned."   *Song of Solomon 8:6-7 KJV*

References

Aristoteles., & Irwin, T. (2007). Nicomachean ethics (2nd ed.). Hackett.

Brown, B. (2010). The Gifts of Imperfection. Hazelden.

Brown, B. (2015). Daring greatly: How the courage to be vulnerable transforms the way we live, love, parent, and lead. Avery, an imprint of Penguin Random House.

Brown, B. (2015). Daring greatly: How the courage to be vulnerable transforms the way we live, love, parent, and lead. Avery, an imprint of Penguin Random House.

Buettner, D. (2010). The blue zones: Lessons for living longer from the people who've lived the longest. National Geographic Society.

Byron, G. G. B., & McGann, J. J. (2008). The Major Works. Oxford University Press.

Chapman, G. D. (2015). The 5 love languages: The secret to love that lasts. Northfield.

Chapman, G. D. (2015). The 5 love languages: The secret to love that lasts. Northfield.

Chapman, G. D. (2015). The 5 love languages: The secret to love that lasts. Northfield.

Cloud, H., & Townsend, J. S. (2012). Boundaries: When to say yes, how to say no to take control of your life (Revised edition. ed.). Zondervan Books.

Cloud, H., & Townsend, J. S. (2012). Boundaries: When to say yes, how to say no to take control of your life (Revised edition. ed.). Zondervan Books.

Coleridge, S. T., & Jackson, H. J. (2008). Samuel Taylor Coleridge: The major works. Oxford University Press.

Covey, S. R. (2004). The 7 Habits of Highly Effective People (Rev. ed.). Free Press.

Covey, S. R. (2006). The Speed of Trust: The One Thing That Changes Everything.

Dweck, C. S. (2016). Mindset: The new psychology of success. Ballantine Books.

Dweck, C. S. (2016). Mindset: The new psychology of success. Ballantine Books.

Enright, R. D. (2012). The Forgiving Life: a Pathway to Overcoming Resentment and Creating a Legacy of Love.

Gottman, J., & DeClaire, J. (2002). The Relationship Cure: A 5-Step Guide to Strengthening Your Marriage, Family, and Friendships. Harmony.

Gottman, J. M., & Silver, N. (2015). The Seven Principles for Making Marriage Work (2nd ed.). Harmony Books.

Gottman, J. M., & Silver, N. (2015). The Seven Principles for Making Marriage Work (2nd ed.). Harmony Books.

Heath, C., & Heath, D. (2013). Made to stick: Why some ideas survive and others die. Random House.

Isay, J. (2008). Walking on Eggshells: Navigating the Delicate Relationship Between Adult Children and Parents.

Johnson, S. (2008). Hold me tight: Seven conversations for a lifetime of love. Little, Brown.

Levitin, D. (2020). This is your brain on music: Understanding a human obsession. Penguin.

Lewis, C. S. (2001). A grief observed, C.S. Lewis. HarperCollins.

Marano, H. E. (2008). A nation of wimps: The high cost of invasive parenting. Broadway Books.

Martin, R. A. (2011). The psychology of humor: An integrative approach (2011 ed.). Elsevier.

Mirivel, J. C. (2021, October 30). Positive Communication: 6 Simple Tips for Success. Help Guide. https://ombuds.columbia.edu/sites/default/files/content/pics/30%20Anniv/The%20Six%20Keys%20to%20Positive%20Communication.pdf

Nelson, S. (2016). Frientimacy: How to deepen friendships for lifelong health and happiness. Seal Press.

Patterson, K., Grenny, J., McMillan, R., & Switzler, A. (2013). Crucial conversations: Tools for talking when stakes are high (2nd ed.). McGraw-Hill.

Peale, N. V. (2015). The power of positive thinking. Touchstone/Simon & Schuster.

Rogers, C. R. (1995). A way of being (9th ed.). Houghton Mifflin.

Rosenberg, M. B. (2015). Nonviolent communication: A language of life (3rd ed.). Puddle Dancer Press.

Rubin, G. (2010). The happiness project. Harper Paperbacks.

Singer, P., & Mason, J. (2007). The ethics of what we eat: Why our food choices matter. Rodale.

Walton, A., Ph.D. (2017). The Empty Quiver, A Journey from The Pain of Despair And Loss To Recovery, Hope And Victory. Walton Publishing

Notes

Notes

Notes

Notes